Looking into Trees
Poems

Douglas Lochhead

Books & Chapbooks by Douglas Lochhead

The Heart is Fire *(1959)*
An old woman looks out on Gabarus Bay ... *(1959)*
It Is All Around *(1960)*
A & B & C &: An Alphabet *(1969)*
Millwood Road Poems *(1970)*
Prayers in a Field: Ten Poems *(1974)*
The Full Furnace: Collected Poems *(1975)*
High Marsh Road *(1980)*; *in Italian,* La Strada di Tantramar *(2004)*
A&E *(1980)*, A&E. *rev. ed. (1998)*
The Panic Field: Prose Poems *(1984)*
Tiger in the Skull: New and Selected Poems *(1986)*
The Red Jeep and Other Landscapes *(1987)*
Upper Cape Poems *(1989)*
Dykelands (With Thaddeus Holownia) *(1989)*
Black Festival: A Long Poem *(1991)*
Homage to Henry Alline and Other Poems *(1992)*
Breakfast at Mel's and Other Poems of Love and Places *(1997)*
All Things Do Continue: Poems *(1997)*
Millwood Road Poems *(1998)*
The Lucretius Poems *(1998)*
Cape Enrage: Poems on a Raised Beach *(2000)*
Orkney: October Diary *(2002)*
Weathers: Poems New & Selected *(2002)*
Midgic *(2003)*
That Place by Tantramar: Sackville, New Brunswick *(2007)*
Love on the Marsh *(2008)*
Looking into Trees: Poems *(2009)*
Letters from Helen (Editor) *(2010)*

Looking into Trees
Poems

Douglas Lochhead

Illustrations by
Kenneth Lochhead

SYBERTOOTH INC
SACKVILLE, NEW BRUNSWICK

Litteris Elegantis Madefimus

The cover features "At Burnet" by Kenneth Lochhead, in the
collection of Douglas Lochhead. The publishers wish to thank Joanne
Lochhead for permission to reproduce the interior illustrations, and for
kindly providing slides of a number of Kenneth Lochhead's works.
Grateful acknowledgement is made to the publishers of *Descant*, in
volume 123 of which four of these poems first appeared, and to the St.
Thomas Poetry Series, publishers of *All Things Do Continue* (1997),
which included "Exhibits for the Lord".

Published by:

> Sybertooth Inc.
> 59 Salem Street
> Sackville, NB
> E4L 4J6
> Canada
> www.sybertooth.ca

The paper is this edition is acid-free and meets all ANSI standards
for archival quality.

Library and Archives Canada Cataloguing in Publication

Lochhead, Douglas, 1922-
     Looking into trees / Douglas Lochhead ; illustrations by Kenneth
Lochhead.

Poems.
ISBN 978-0-9810244-3-1

     I. Lochhead, Kenneth, 1926-2006 II. Title.

PS8523.O33L66 2009   C811'.54   C2009-903754-8

Contents

I

a new morning ...9
Apple   ...10
Boss man   ...12
Dream perchance   ...13
From the Deck   ...14
From the top   ...18
Hi neighbour   ...19
In the heart of the stone   ...20
Leavings   ...21
Listen   ...22
Much to be said   ...23
Never mind   ...24
New evidence   ...25
sky   ...26
Sudden beginning   ...27
Tantramar River   ...28
The enjoyment of now   ...29
The long mysteries   ...31
The long nuisance   ...32
The river's time   ...33
The sea-gate   ...34
Wild bird   ...37
You understand? ...38

II

looking into trees   ...40
In the woods   ...41
Light recession   ...42
November love   ...45
Noon light   ...48
Tall stages   ...49
Concerto grosso   ...51

III

At last!   ...58
The wind in Sackville   ...60
A happy dance   ...61
Exhibits for the Lord: North Toronto   ...62
A dream   ...66
long love poem   ...67
Love suite   ...70
Objects in a garden   ...75
The wave itself   ...76
Letter I - II - III   ...77
The catch   ...81
Questions in Sackville   ...85
Love, I mean   ...86
Snow Devils   ...87
Our Darkness   ...88

IV

Thoughts on a New Year's morning on a
stricken beach   ...90

Paintings by Ken Lochhead

At Burnet   ...front cover
Fall Arboretum 2 (2000) *detail   ...8*
Cathedra Light (1994) *detail   ...17*
Tall Stages (1997) *detail   ...39*
Concerto Grosso (1995) *detail   ...57*
Late Fall Arboretum (2006) *detail   ...89*
Autumn Pattern (1994) *detail   ...100*

About the Author and Illustrator   ...101

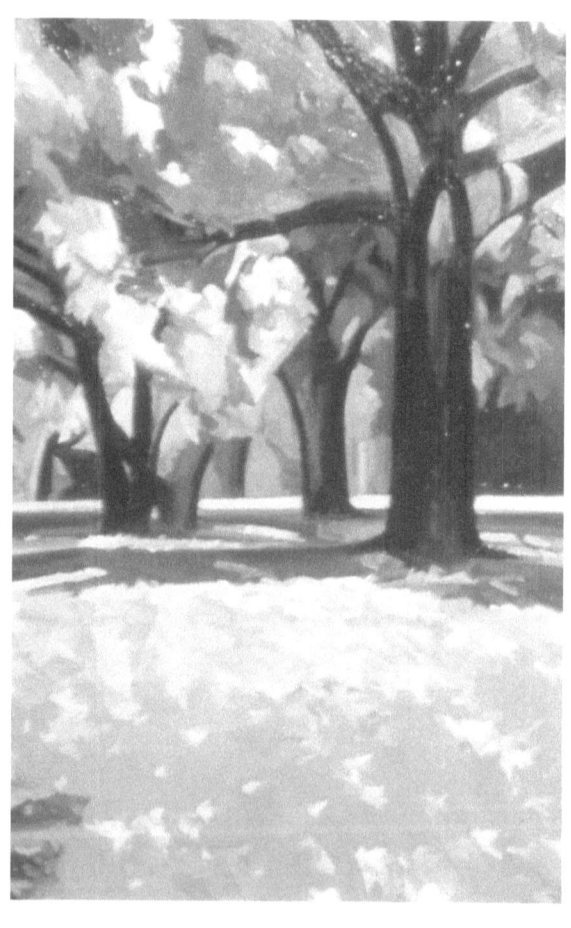

Fall Arboretum 2 (2000)
(detail)

I

a new morning

the simple pleasure.
life lying damp
on a new morning

our hands as leaves
find a fresh lift
of light

there are new turnings
new embraces
on a new morning

Apple

apple
I hold you

we have
a relationship

how old
are you

apple
of red cheeks?

I hear
you say

you have
many lives

your hanging,
your fall

what next?
I ask.

your sudden
translations

lie down
before us

like the plum
there is

an ongoing
drama

quiet play
of moves

of earth's
gestures

open wide
dear apple

show and tell
your deep treasures.

Boss man

I have taken over the hours,
appropriated the minutes, seconds,
the days look after themselves

details, facts, to place on the table
arrange them in rows for counting
to keep this place straight, narrow

& heavy with order, I will put down
the breathing works as they happen, &
throw and broadcast them as poems.

Dream perchance

He said: 'Look over there, over there'
and I went to see, perchance to find,

but there was nothing, nothing to see
and he had gone, walking fast I'm sure

so that the blue mountain, the tumbled clouds,
the grave city in the long shadows

were all that remained. It was curious,
because no voices, no shrieks or groans arose

to make a place of it, only the levelled dream,
a flowing together of someone in a foreign space.

From the Deck

I

here, right here, where I find myself
in a chair with catalogue name

of 'Gracious Living' I hear wilder signals
from the deck, wilder than before

and looking into great ranges of hemlock,
spruce, and maple, I see, no, I feel

the vibes of the great task, say it again,
that noble move of life in such trees

where in the three by five freedom
of eyes looking out, the growth thing,

not far removed and entangled with
the age thing, call it daily maintenance

the step of hope, having given up hope
and feeling much better, I decide

to be commander for a day, this deck
is sailing where it ought to sail

over a Moby Dick sea, white nothing,
no tail showing and you can say that

again, making laughter a private medicine,
a sort of looking down the forest's throat.

14   *Douglas Lochhead*

II

it is getting into the slur and sound
of telling & speaking, confessing a part

here, a spare there, intimate for public
consumption, that's intimate (?) But

it is how it must have been with a
momma and a poppa, Toots and George,

but these came, the names later,
Toots, unlikely comic-strip echo

while George is the ploughman bent
with just being around to pay bills

and in the later years, 389 Third
Avenue in the Ottawa Glebe, so it was

on leaving there in peace and war and peace
T. would wave a musician woman's hand

while G. standing beside her, would
place left hand to nose and right

hand in the air going down for
the final time with one rich guffah

which led to his deathbed oration
later, later, 'thanks for the buggy-ride'

as twenty-four hour nurses for which
they really saved wheeled his wheelèd ship.

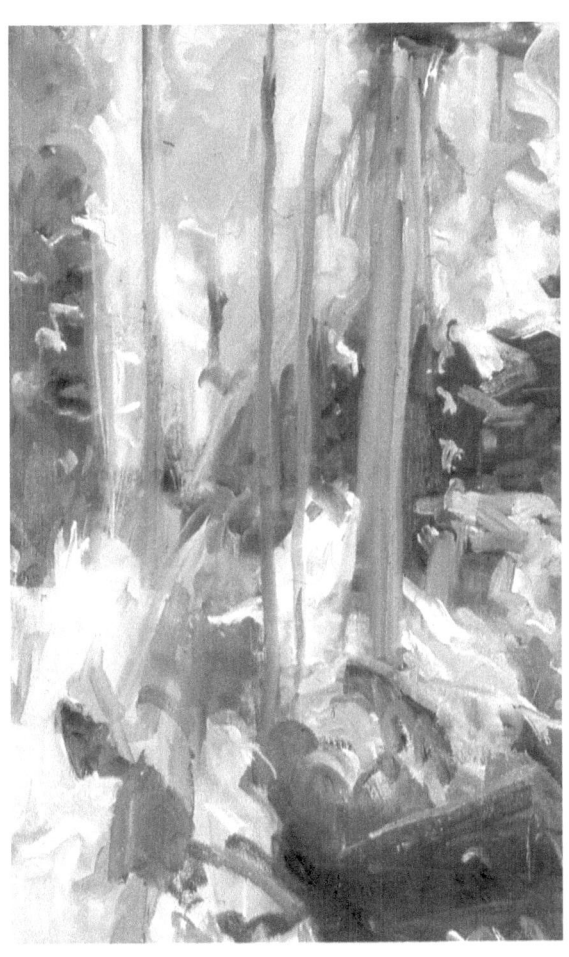

Cathedra Light (1994)
(detail)

From the top

from the top
looking into the betweens
of light and shadow
the eye climbs down
the body
(stopping first at breasts
moving out from branches)
really a long pause
then, if lucky, down
to roots, to limbs
of grass (here we are)
now to look up
seeing it all again
another way.

Hi neighbour

My friend the bee, humble-bumble, busy
   to you, now hear this softly,
      a lisp of love for you and envy
         watching you come as close
            as you do to the face
               to the very lip of that flower
                  that rose.

Your new quarters I hear are under
   this place, porch, call it deck,
      the patient flying in and out
         is part of possession, well,
            fix it up, build a roof,
               spend the night, find food
                  in that beautiful rose
                     right there.

In the heart of the stone

love in the heart
    of the stone
in awakening clouds
    finding their way
into the arms of the morning,
    from the lips
of lovers moving where stars
    find themselves
and their new glow breeds more love
    in the heart of the stone.

Leavings

Tossed up by storms of winter
leavings of vanished fleets
lie along the raised beach;

lost planks from Spanish fishers
torn by winds on foreign oceans
thrown wide for sea to swallow,

so go the turnings of our days
the hot flashes of love and life
the long ropes and spars tethering us.

Yes, we are tied by love to one another
in the rock and sway of arms and legs
just as leavings on the world's beach.

Listen

life
is listening

is finding
sounds

is feeling
rhythms

in all
things

life
is waiting

is standing
here and there

is saying
words

is praying
everywhere

Much to be said

There is much to be said
much to be listened to

going out from here the waves
bring messages to the outer sea

your lips are like the waves
they send prayers across the waters

your words become ships, who
is to chart their far voyages?

Or have they come home to rest,
to bring new tales for me?

Never mind

Never mind about strong men,
it is a time for weeping, for the soul
to bring itself together in the wind,
for taking on a new skin for old bones
to find a place for silent weeping
for a spell.

It is beyond telling, no story mouths itself,
I sit on the black rock of my being and undoing,
against the sea of my deception and deceit
the afternoon of clouds parades my world of woe,
the half-eyed glint from a broken beast
unfolds it all.

Now to start, to unwind a new beginning,
to let it be. A new song finds its place upon the
        lips,
words fly in unexpected ways, the touch of skin
becomes a brilliant moment, a rose reveals itself,
the smell of it fares wide upon the land,
a white rock rises from the sea.

New evidence

the slow, drawn out confessions of the aged
who wants to hear them?

the question lingers but the story grows,
it takes over for a while

coughing and clearing, he said he wasn't here
to offer wisdoms, coloured insights,

no, he was really here to raise a banner
to lay the groundwork for a celebration

to report that there were surprises
would be close to the way it was

to be witness to his smile and ways of prayer
to move with care into his breathing times

so it was new evidence from old sources,
something to take home, his smiles, his silences.

sky

eyes
reach
into pure
distances
of white
and blue
parades

there is
now
a marriage
of calm
a summer's
warm
embrace

and as
sky
enfolds
river
woods
in its
moving arms
pilgrims
sleep

Sudden beginning

Go on.
No, I really mean it.
Well then let's sit down
and figure it out.

Do you see that door?
Yes, I see that door
It has a handle.
Well, then turn the knob
see what happens to it, to you

There I applied a little pressure
and turned the knob,
then a little push and voilà
it swung on its hinges.
So what do I do now?

You see before you a new world
a wide glorious landscape
a new place to think about
that striking bed is your universe
your sudden beginning.

Tantramar River

At Cookville
many streams
innocent, pure, gather
into pools Monet
would have taken
for his own
petal strewn
and lasting
as each day
the river runs

it is a dividing glory
through marsh fields,
a bridge or two
a stretching time
through lost country
known a century ago
but quiet now

until the sea noise
is heard and lost
in tidal moments
the Tantramar
grows and turns
singing its final song.

The enjoyment of now

the enjoyment of now
under the bough
bearing apples:

every word is suspect:
enjoyment.

You and whatever
you have it
in your mind
to call me

every work is suspect:
mind.

yes, we are alike
as nothing we
have seen or heard,
telling it aloud
to the watching sun
to the watching sea

how much we assume:
watching, waiting.

yes, all of nature
waves a field
of hands,
a billowed cloud
and all,
so we do go through
reaching for hands
yours and mine
the one the other

just missing,
missing, missing.

The long mysteries

The long mysteries:
a snake-trail
through life's jungle,

there is the drum-beat
the urgent thunder
the lost sea-faces

once I stopped
and reached for dust
but my past blew it away

only when I looked
into the face of today
did stars laugh
and the sun shine on me.

The long nuisance

the long nuisance of winter
yes, it has come to that

forgetting the rain bit, let us take
the nights, they are easy to find

and the story goes there is more love
made in the snow months than, say,

spring and summer, some would even say
the fall lacks any sign of fire

so we are locked in with each other
do I detect something in this squeezing dark?

The river's time

out there the river as rogue
    its long blue (today) fever
    of spring

this is its take-over time
    turning muscles through green silk
    of awakening trees

there is a hill chorus, beeches
    and maples, deep elms,
    the thin echoes, rustle

over there deeper green edges
    pursue the flood-time, the river's
    winter dream unfolds

it is the river's time unleashing
    harsh tongues of ice, blue water
    with white cheeks

the song of revival, of slumber recovery
    of prayers laid upon mountains
    the voice of the river saying a prayer
    forever, ever.

The sea-gate

I

the sea-gate opens:
    a wide game of gulls
    chasing themselves, following
    the far-out tide, winks
    of light against brown,
    brown sand
    and, over there
the rocks tumble into themselves
hard crumbled edges
on their way to more pebbles
    and sand.

II

the stage lies (all the world)
before us
now the eye finds
the long join of sky,
a forever moving thing,
a mute drama
waiting to be found.

III

given light, a pass of shadow,
the face of stone, a beard of sand,
    an outwash fan

the beach out of the melting,
Ice Age leavings

the same waiting continues
into life's image
of sorts.

IV

take the cliff:
it is a waiting crumble,
a leaning into air,
a spruce held as hostage
strange appendage
a curved leaning laugh

a hair, long, left
on a shaved face
it waits for its roots to go,
it waits for the light
of afternoon.

V

not much of a moon,
a dull pitch
a give or take moment,

there are stars
lying in the ditch
what strange calculations
calamities

so that time, the present,
rings itself wild
with more than sea sounds.

Wild bird

yes,

I hear you
wild bird

standing tall
out there

where marsh
and sea

dance together
in their quiet

and rousing
ways

look at you
look at me

caught up
in our silent watch
and worship.

You understand?

You understand?
Of course you understand.
Look at it this way
    or that way

take it as is,
for the first time
taste and swallow it.
try to remember it
    but not too hard
it will never be the same
again

but, don't you see,
there is music in the sand
in the stones lying there
or rolling
and the all-day, all-night
symphony
is all around

feel it on your shoulders
let it linger on your forehead
go down with it
along the landscape
of your body

feel its feet
    in the forest
    all around you.

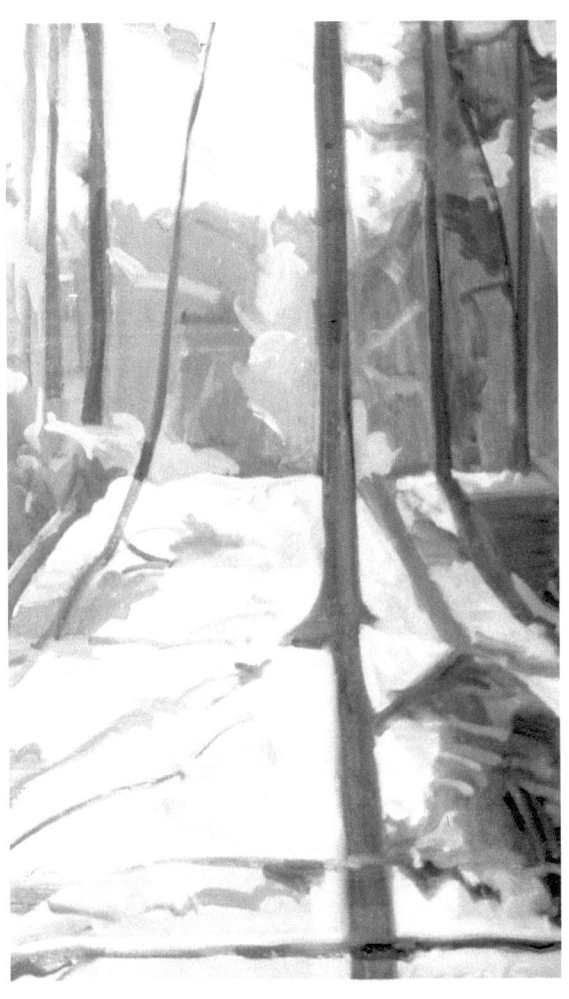

Tall Stages (1997)
(detail)

II

looking into trees

refusing to see faces
(impossible in this wind
this moment)
there in the vacancies.
the spaces of seconds
the crazy or controlled
crossings of the green place
the flashed-out leaves
make a dizzy wall
before our eyes.

Go wind, go green, go move it
into great shiftings.

In the woods

Well, it's over there
the woods, the trees
the shrubs and weeds
the whole growing, greening
     thing

so that you will see it
the rain falls
and captures every leaf
a new and glistening paint job

and, of course, there is
     music
(it needs a line unto itself)
crazy and simple birds
sing songs, together and apart
and, then there are the resident
     squirrels
leaping over bending branches
heading (tailing) somewhere
to take their places
in the woods, the woods

darkness, then light, lifted places
by winds and snows
an interior of sorts
a leading into darkness
so do the woods breathe
and go green and other colours
in everlasting light.

Light recession

1

There are turnings
    slow and sudden reaches
    into the forest

2

little high drama
    no climbing
    no fences

3

the long smoke of days
    hangs loose and heavy
    along the path

4

let us walk in
    brushing aside
    yesterday's traces

5

take my hand
    if you like
    if you need me

6

why do I feel
    the forest's warmth
    its green beckoning?

7

this is not the dead land
    the dark
    and voiceless place

8

sounds wait to be heard
    a white still
    pervades

9

see, a long limp of light
    trails between trees
    through there

10

here life sleeps somehow
    in white dreams
    of woods and snow.

November love

1

it came in fast,
it moved
without noise
except for gifts
of wind and rain

2

weather report
of love and loss
of quick moves
into deep talk
of hot and cold

3

now we tremble
as trees, as shrubs
the colour is rust,
a burnt face
along edges

4

in the forest
there is openness
a reaching in
of eyes where leaves
are curtains drawn close

5

before there was
a festival of fire
a new design
taken over
from a summer's green

6

yes, a quiet party now,
a blending
of new branches,
a shaking, sharing
of new forest limbs

7

do you, my love,
take these in,
these warm arms
of seasons, of life
in this close wrapped time?

8

the forest is a sharing
of November leaves
long limbers of delight
where dreams share
a glowing fire of love and life.

Noon light

The round power
of your limbs
the quiet rush
into spring green

places beginning
to grow higher
the clean silence
of cathedrals

the assumption
of summer
a crowd waving
in flag-layers

there are late reds
and veins of gold
fall's fusillade
the surprise of fire

there is the pursuit
of seasons
stark unveiling
for winter's eyes.

Tall stages

It was
our time
to enter
the forest
primeval
the tall stages
the long
high
drippings

where we walked
almost
as prisoners
willing lopers
in chains
reaching
from tree
to tree

it was
the dark green
centre
of the world
but
with sudden
lights

and it was
(as well
we knew it)
our past
and dripping
present,
the forest.

Concerto grosso

1

beyond and within
unlikely marriage
there is the cry
of distance

concerto grosso
forest dialogue

2

to see the forest
is recognition
of depth

light's magic
undoes the place

3

winter's presence:
there are new hollows
new comings
silent pilings

4

storm:
white death
in a surfeit
of wind
a forest withdrawn

5

drifts
beyond measure
stark sensation
of white words
gone cold

6

realm of white
holding place
waiting out
the day
the night

7

to enter:
the eyes tell
beginnings
of innocence

arms move
as silent
branches

8

it all warms
in a lift of light
white bandages
of January snow

there is a telling
to be heard
together

9

a private exhibition
instruments of love
yes, my dear.
a beginning

concerto grosso

10

as love
in slow beginnings
when life
is all beginnings

flurries appear
in tentative fall

11

reach into me
please stay

my coming
is felt
only by you
it is a meeting

12

words as flakes
as snow falling
into white spaces

there are messages
somewhere
to be heard

13

a certain ceremony
of love's parade
lifts your face
for me to see

a kind of worship

14

the day's escape:
to become lost
where trees are fences
where a lapse of winter
undoes our spaces
and limbs embrace
in new discovery

15

now, to watch
full flare of light
down avenues
of white

16

to dark stations
into broken limps
of hemlock
it is our way in
to intimate
forest places

17

it is our love
of deep contrasts
of lost light
of night design
of dark enclosure

18

listen
now there is music
sudden whispers
then soft drums
leaning branches
a forest dance
concerto grosso.

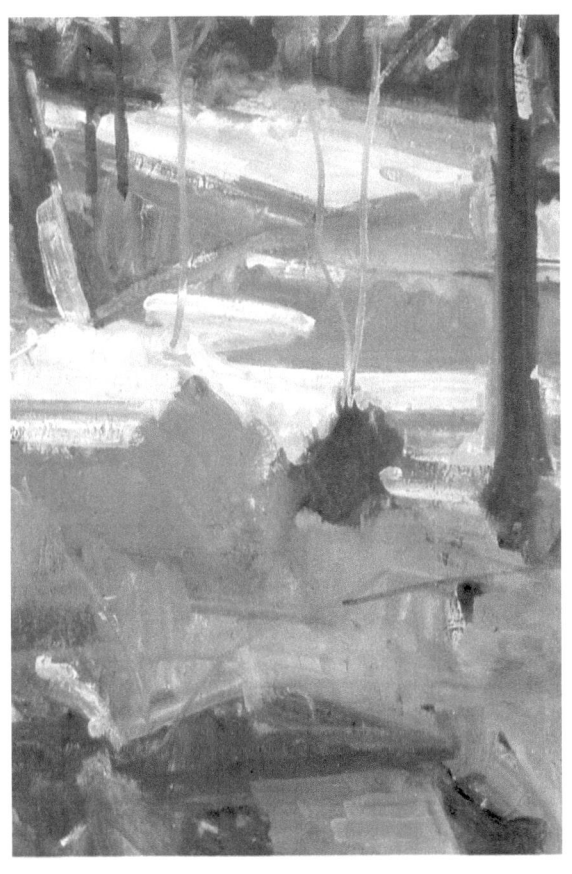

Concerto Grosso (1995)
(detail)

III

At last!

The old codger
came by
slowly

one foot,
pause,
then the other

what else
had he
to do

but count
the clouds
up there

and amble
and take
it easy

but this day
he felt
funny

there was
a pain
in chest

he sat down
right there
and smiled

he said
to help me
at last!

The wind in Sackville

The wind
in Sackville
makes a noise

every day
at five
o'clock

you can set
your clock
one man said

the first signs
are in
the hemlocks

their branches
bounce and lean
and wave

and you know,
Sackville knows,
it is five o'clock.

A happy dance

Take my hand
my dear
or I'll take yours

and we will
dance
a happy dance

out there
across the lawn
along the path

see, look,
others join us
with happy smiles

it is catching
an epidemic
of dancing
and happiness.

Exhibits for the Lord - North Toronto

I

bright morning. bright evening
thanks, thanks, my brief wedge of life
turns with the wind of your directions
it breathes sparks like dandelions
this spring session of prayers and processions
to walk to work down Glengrove Avenue
in the timing of forsythia, daffs, tulips
all in fine order of lawns, robin flights
making invisible landings, great colours
of windows for eyes, for shadows
when so much is said without saying
except when we read it on face of sky,
in firming shapes to heaven as buds shove
out making faces, exhibits for the Lord.

Exhibits for the Lord - North Toronto

II

procession I saw of children, taut drama
where the hedge of barberry shunts them in
or exit stopping stamping in urgency
of whatever is in them
Thanks, thanks
praying for them from a window
of middle age where joy grows sometimes
in the shrub of me not yet gone to wood
but out of wet winter-gone earth
branches in surprise of love, of time
it being today as every when I
taste a tongue of rejoicing, a whisper,
growth into hosannahs, make it
a halelujah, cheers in the subway,
and because children walked this way, this way.

Exhibits for the Lord - North Toronto

III

great while before day and into slippers
of prayer downstairs to drowse with Agatha Christie
the only way in the space of morning
in the queer dark, the avenue a tension
of unseen sleepers while I found light
and words took me up saying REJOICE
and it was God's day again already
what in the burning tongue told me to pray
and find cool waters lying in them face down
in the frantic state of wakefulness
induction at 2:40 to a devout life
did Hopkins ever smile? no similarity.
only the possibility of dappled smiles
to share in the close silence of morning before birds.

Exhibits for the Lord - North Toronto

IV

today I will become a jogger only
on my knees finding in quiet and silence
the rule and exercises of Holy Living
the slide rule possibility of Holy dying
where the daily trot to town to work
brings one to humble reflection
I think of Trollope sitting in railway carriage
moving his pen and beard and mind
in envious rhythm growing as he wrote
into habit of talk and mouthing sounds
for me of praise and nevermind
what else drives the pidgeon from its perch
but the devout life, is whatever
the jog-jog of day thoughts says, it says
      REJOICE.

A dream

First a dream of meadows:
loose happenings of sleep,
the way of grasses opens
until a stage of sky
appears

it is a wide welcome
a happy dream along the way
where wide margins meet
and there are dreamers' steps
leading here and here

yes, it is a place for younger days
platform of light and happenings
openings everywhere
crows stitch clouds together
a temple emerges

now, a vanished dream:
wide expanse, a frozen place
deserted except for this old man
sad but grinning survivor
waiting to tell his story.

long love poem

you
will
be
here
when
I
return

let
it
be
so

we
will
set
the
margins
of
our
life

or
will
we
accept
them
as
they
come

it
is
for
you
to
decide

it
is
for
us
to
live
this
way
up
against
the
margins
within
the
arms
of
love.

Love Suite

1
a deep miracle
a recognition
unanimous

2
the ultimate now
coming together
out of a touch,
the eye's corner

3
come away, no,
we will stay
where there is cover
where we will hide

4
it was right
a fair weather
in all constellations
in God's house

5
the natural world
the cleansed universe
the slow motion
of our joining

6
a rainbow!
you embraced it
the confirmation
of prayer, of time's
arch of colour

7
a heron followed
down ways of brook
its presence a kind
of sign, deliverance

8
look, we are together
in a wonder of love
happy entreaties
of joy

9
your eyes unfold
showing laughter
there are sighs
little miracles of sound

10
the sea binds us
limp waves encompass
hands, feet, legs
reaching, reaching
into your embracing caves

11
a touch of sky
with clouds as banners
filling the distance
of our enduring present

12
the importance of fingers
the touch tells
messages spill over
from the grip of it

13
my head, your shoulder
a moment swells
into a recognition
of forever

14
your hair reaching
for the waist, a sweep
of it bares the neck
where I kiss, kiss

15
love is a dance
turns spring loose
there is continuing
celebration

16
new words fly
over the simmering bed
little ploys and ploys of mirth
music, music, music

17
time, what is time?
love is past counting
wild birds come
in strange seasons

18
our expeditions lean
into the unknown
where the warm forest
of your mound
breeds wild fires

19
the landscape of your back
its calm and waiting place
harbours new sighs
new tales of ecstasies
to come

20
I love you, I really do
those are my very words
what we say into our eyes
is for all lovers.

Objects in a garden

    white
the white chair
    white garden chair

    green
the green lawn
    green hedge
  of cedars

    brown
the brown fence
    we paid
    and Mr. Cahill built
    brown fence

    black
the black elm
    black tree
    two-three hundred years
    black tree

    around which, all,
    the wind is voice
    shadow
    it and elm

    and white
    and green
    and brown
    and black

The wave itself

It has taken
forty-nine years
to recognize
the absolute need
for one blanket
to cover me
that is, to believe
in details
the little signs
the blue flags
waving
touching the wave
at sea-edge
and
the wave itself

Letter One

So you will be and I
caught in my own ambush
of words to cough out
this letter to you. To You.
Yes, and the fair walking
into the morning mystery,
the marsh seeks a figure
to set in its own landscape.
From here I settle down
close with bee and bird,
how close to love, because
it really is. So here I am
doing my dance in a quiet place
the sun early sending, and I
place my word, then another,
and where the salt-hay grows
the pile of them continues. They
are there, piled dreams gone out
in a set V of geese following
the Fundy shore, so do they go
out that way to you.

Letter Two

There is no placed time, only
the past of silences, the moving
in dyked waters, the flash
of words and wing, the taking
off into thunder, into storm,
into winds rising from west
where the weight of it all
grows heavy with feeling,
with the wonder of you
and the steps we took
following the red ruts hard
going out and on.

P.S. This is my place and I
will tell you more,
God giving. O roll this
pleasure blistering on.

Letter Three

No, it is my own burning
filling the crushed air
and what I salvage
is the burnt hurt
and another mystery.

Go flame, blacken fields
in false hope of new growth
the staring day blinds
in the heat of noon,
the tapering time spins
a blanket of black
where comes the count
of crazy unseen clocks
the heart burns itself
in the breast's counting.

Do you feel it? The fire
in the baking time turns
on its own spit, the body
creaks in a crackle of skin,
the brain leaks, the singe
of smoke lies low on the place
and the helpless bird
only fans the thirsting flame.
Yes, we run now from it
the heart is scant saving
but the bitter scent
the taking gesture of flame
wraps our trail and love
speaks a cold song.

Now it is this way
the raging heat gives tongues,
we must live to taste
to bite in such places
where the telling is
the place gone wild
and the crazy fire
is our own making
all around, around us.

The Catch

I

Coming out into the open
        the place widens
                        to plains
        but close up, there,
        in the flat waters
the facts lie open wide
        below us
        like shells
        their order almost visible
        the poem itself
        waiting
        to be taken in
You, Clutch, Harry Clutch, go back
        look over the place
        and see what
        has been forgotten.
        I have that feeling
        and we shall wait
        our feet by the beached dory
        at Hippo Rock
there is some shadow

II

the going will be tough
          because of the month it is
          all of the way
Clutch, in the way of things
          we should be there
          and without so much
          you will take off
          to find that black-haired
          one of Mrs. Schilling, or,
          the Missus herself,
          only a little teasing
          against the kitchen table
          after sitting most
          of the evening
          rolling Vogue
          both a little beer-full
          and all of your stalling talk
and then it will be
          the way
          you both want it
          the way you told me
          once before
nothing like love on oilcloth
          no stage, only the view
          where a man in the harbour
          goes down nord
          to his mooring
          earlier than birds
there will be time
          to sit around *The Pilot*

on the way back
and the burnt-out
                    veterans
will come in
giving way
to others
we knew his trespass
        when you looked out
        seeing him
        and getting hope
        wretch-eyed
        on the kitchen table
        Clutch, boy,
        piss on the person,
        he doesn't understand you.

III

poet all in one breath
        the tide turns around
        and testing you run with it
        pulling a poem out
        the wild dory sway
        in your bully-mind
the sea-sock of a storm
        takes its shrieks
        from our faces
        but the poem flips,
                        is sealed,

lies limping
ready to be eaten
by some inshore bastard
Yes, it is a damn net-catch
      holed by ourselves
      as we turn into touch
      and push water back
      for harbour.

Questions in Sackville

There it is
the Town Clock
at the corner
of Bridge and Main

against background
of town buildings
including
the Council Chambers
and important offices

but the Town Clock
has stopped,
it is without
its customary smile,
its story to tell

but in Sackville
who cares?
bless it.
what is time
anyway?
and why?

Love, I mean

It is not enough
love, I mean:

love reaching so far
then, in a wind, taking off
into what realms
of other pleasures;

love turning into its own depths
into far fathoms of other colours
soft pressures
in such secret places

our embrace waits
a long lifting of arms and soul
holding there for none to see
will tears be enough?

Snow Devils

in the afternoon light
a field of snow devils
coiled and caught explosions
spread on a frozen field of snow

the light enwraps them
prepares them for a secret dance
a cold caper about to unfold
what forces continue to breed them.

Our Darkness

I

Darkness   lost spaces   time
of searching   say, for the black rules,
divisions   now let us reach   for the margins
for they are there   but invisible   time
for resolutions   age   the multiple years
speaking of darkness

II

let us roll   into each other   finding
close pleasures   your damp warmth
turns to fire   first beacon   white place
new country   dark makings   hands
as first probes   searches   for
a sleeping sun

III

our warmth blossoms   night flowers   sly perfumes
embrace us   let us find our lips   wet touch
there is your little forest   forgotten dark
our heaving is like the sea   host of rogue waves
the bed our beach   lapping music
a losing darkness   a beginning rhapsody of light.

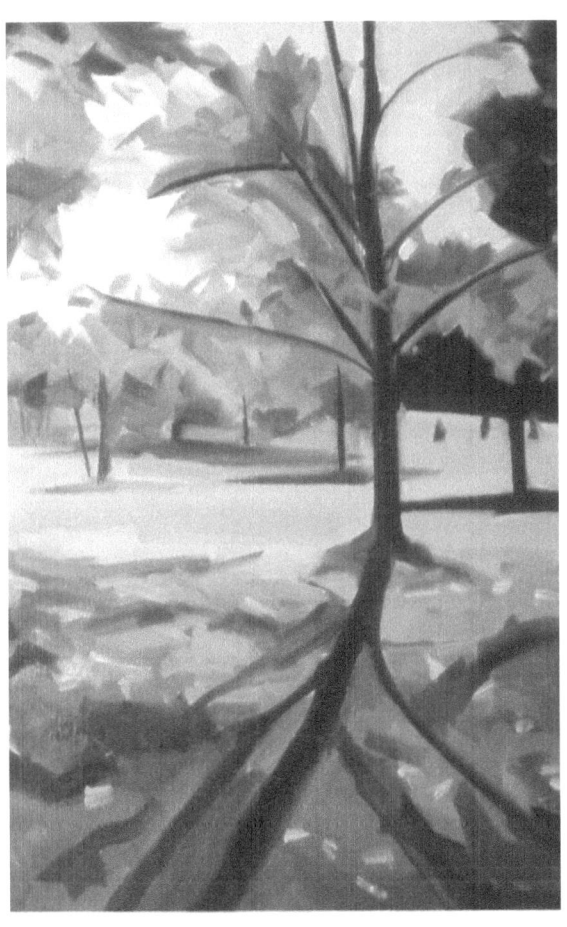

Late Fall Arboretum (2006)
(detail)

IV

Thoughts on a New Year's Morning on a Stricken Beach Aberlady, Scotland

I

this be
this be it
I said, said I
a raw run
take
memory
through
a winding dark
a stricken beach it is
in a bare length
of rolling
sand, stone
surf
great breakers
galloping
into my
tossed whatever

II

yes, I said
it be just
that
and what
goes wild
is dance
pure throat
love giving
way
to heebie-
jeebies
(you know
the kind)
there to
be told
not listed
like groceries
things done
not undone
so that
the gulf
gives wide
and between
rocks
slowly
becomes
itself
a safe place

III

subject
I always said
rocking the while
to change
you might say
but wild
storm and
not so storm
the sliding
place
for moments
before fires
where not
enough time
is spent
is captured
quiet
the face
burning
in you
and me
you tell it
an easy thing
so that
when I sing
a drunk hymn
to heaven
the way is
ready
the sea feels

it's our hymn
the broken
lines
slip into
startled air
but you never
gonna let it go

IV

no, praise it
always
praise it
with your hands
like this
and what
is said
your words
they 'elp
you
bend your
bows
five arrows
into bellies
of cloud
letting the rain
follow the river
I can see
storms
ripping down
the Ottawa
the valley
with vanished

rafts, logs
the Irish booms
slipping seals
down kettles
of rock
sluice 'er
through
my potatoes
men
giffer a go
from past
counties
there's plenty
where that
comes from
me boyo bye

V

sewing this way
the cloth
makes
its own pattern
giving girth
to what
or was not
or somewhere
in between
giving
a stage
of truth
so close
is it cut

and
so wide
so
various-vested
the night is
at that:
Coleridge
where did you
find
that one?
you could
only have been
a Dragoon
to know
the nights
that way
vests varied
a pleasant change
from masks
but 'hail'
it is
the moon
and visions
all
the
watery-eyed
staring
we do in this
moon-day
and
moon-night
care, despair
moon

a
flashlight
but
Coleridge
at sixteen
fields
autumn moon
like
football
turns it
into world
and makes
sonnet
hail Coleridge

VI

as felt
so conceived
poem is made
I believe
is fitted
morticed
sanded
comes closer
it dies
to what
I aspire to
being truly
a carpenter
with a few
faithful
clients
not waitin'
to tell me
what to do
and when
I pick a tune
and my fiddle
is many varied

vested
in a barnyard
brawl
bringing
a mixture
of swung
jingle bells
and
'Men of Harlech'

VII

O great moment
warm and late
heavy drinks
in a Manse
at Aberlady
and with
three clerics
and one wife
and whisky and fiddling
at two in the morning
we opened
the windows
looking out
to the new year
and the mighty Forth
and bird sanctuary
and the wild chorus
of startled swans
when I gave them
'Men of Harlech'

— true,
so was the warming
pan
in my pudding bed
and I would
have had a chat
with her
but the timing
was off
Hail, Mrs. M
my pure lovelie.

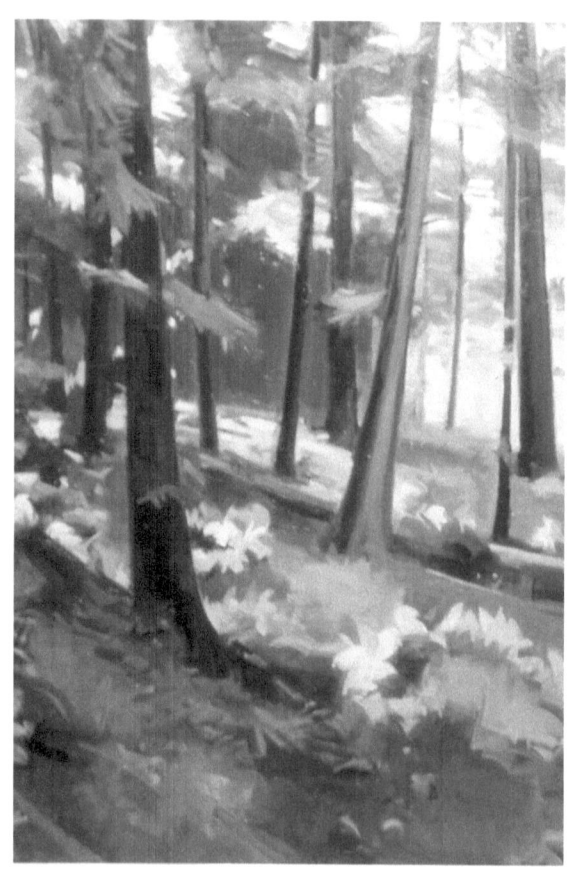

Autumn Pattern (1994)
(detail)

Douglas Lochhead

Douglas Lochhead

A Fellow of the Royal Society of Canada and a life-member of the League of Canadian Poets, he is a graduate of McGill University and the University of Toronto. He has taught English and been a member of the library staffs of universities in Canada, the United States, and Scotland. At Mount Allison University, he has held the positions of Davidson Professor of Canadian Studies and Writer in Residence. A Senior Fellow and Founding Librarian of Massey College, University of Toronto, Lochhead has received the Alden Nowlan Award, the Carlo Betocchi Prize, and several honorary degrees.

Kenneth Lochhead

Ken Lochhead's honours include the Order of Canada, the Golden Jubilee Medal, the Governor General's Award in Visual and Media Arts, and an Honorary Doctor of Laws from the University of Regina. One of the Regina Five painters –leaders in Canada's modern art movement– his work has appeared in more than three hundred national and international exhibitions, and he taught at the University of Manitoba, York University, the University of Saskatchewan, and the University of Ottawa. More about Ken Lochhead can be found online at:

www.kennethlochhead.com

Excerpt from Lochhead's *Love on the Marsh,*
also published by Sybertooth (ISBN 9780973950533)

1.

the marsh:
this is our stage
wide green place
of discovery, of love,
of venturing into caves
where clouds live.

2.

it began with your eyes. bouquet
of two. daisies along the path.
beyond was the sea. summer's fires
were everywhere. petals of love
flew on the marsh wind.
backyard Eden.
this is our place.

3.

forgive me before we say anything.
will we wait for the night? what
do your arms say? I am stranger.
we are young. there are questions.
do you hear me?

4.

the reaching, touching poet.
love lopes in many ways. it is
that splendour of many paths.
it spreads in its curving ways
across the marsh. my love, let's
follow. these are beginnings.

5.

there are decisions. I await
your elucidations. your stolid
one-liners which reach around
this place. the sky as blackboard.
a message of clouds.

6.

take me. take me into your wide
embrace. what are we here for?
you ask. hey, we are here to
celebrate. spell it, please.
L - O - V - E.

Other books published by Sybertooth Inc.
www.sybertooth.ca

Love on the Marsh
By Douglas Lochhead

Poet Douglas Lochhead has been, for over a quarter century, the voice of the Tantramar Marshes. His latest work, *Love on the Marsh*, gives an intimate portrait of the relationship between two lovers set against the unique landscape that Lochhead knows so well.

ISBN-13: 9780973950533
Trade paperback • published 2008

Hitler Versus Me
Volume VIII of the Bandy Papers
By Donald Jack

It's 1940, and the intrepid air ace of WWI is eager to join the fight against Germany. Unfortunately, everyone seems to think Bandy is too old to be flying Spitfires, and should go quietly into retirement to polish his medals and knighthoods. Bandy, however, has other ideas, and uses his friends and/or enemies in high places to manoeuvre himself into the Battle of Britain.

This edition also includes Donald Jack's novelette "Where Did Rafe Madison Go?".

ISBN-13: 9780968802489
Trade paperback • published 2006
$19.00 (Can) • £12.00 (UK) • $16.00 (US)

Stalin Versus Me
Volume IX of the Bandy Papers
Bandy's Last Escapade
By Donald Jack

Gwinny just can't understand why Bandy has been feeling less amorous ever since he was almost convicted of treason as a result of one of her schemes. But love rears its head again, the King needs a man of tact and discretion for a delicate post-war job in Germany, and there's an embarrassing parcel of ladies' undies to explain, not to mention just why a half-clothed Bandy is in bed with George Garanine, that lazy, loveable, failed Bandy-assassin. From Normandy to Brussels to Yalta to Moscow, Bandy's career path is as labyrinthine as ever, strewn with bottles, battles, and brasshat blood-pressure.

ISBN-13: 9780968802472
Trade paperback • published 2005
$18.00 (Can) • £11.00 (UK) • $15.00 (US)

Other books published by Sybertooth Inc.
www.sybertooth.ca

The Captain Star Omnibus
By Steven Appleby
£8.99 UK • $16.00 US • $19.99 CAN
ISBN: 9780973950564 • 146pp
Size: 8.25" x 11" • 28cm x 21cm
From the creator of the cult-classic *Captain Star* TV cartoon series: the
first collection of comic strips tracing the strange but illustrious career
of Captain Jim Star – the greatest hero any world has ever known –
from its surreal beginnings to its improbable middle. Witness his
triumphs, learn from his words of wisdom, and meet his crew on the
Boiling Hell: Navigator Black, Officer Scarlette, and Atomic Engine
Stoker "Limbs" Jones.

K.V. Johansen
The Storyteller and Other Tales – A collection for adults and older
teens, *The Storyteller and Other Tales* will take you on a journey
through exotic worlds and times.

Max Ferguson
And Now ... Here's Max. The Leacock award-winning memoir of his
life at the CBC, by the legendary Max Ferguson. With an introduction
by Shelagh Rogers.

Helen VanWart
Letters from Helen, edited by Douglas Lochhead
A collection of letters and photographs from a New Brunswick girl
travelling to Leipzig, Germany to study music just before the outbreak
of the First World War.